First Facts™

The Solar System

The Moon

by Ralph Winrich

Consultant:
Stephen J. Kortenkamp, PhD
Research Scientist
Planetary Science Institute, Tucson, Arizona

Capstone
press

Mankato, Minnesota

First Facts is published by Capstone Press,
151 Good Counsel Drive, P.O. Box 669, Mankato, Minnesota 56002.
www.capstonepress.com

Library of Congress Cataloging-in-Publication Data
Winrich, Ralph.
    The moon / by Ralph Winrich.
    p. cm.—(First facts. The solar system)
    Includes bibliographical references and index.
    ISBN 0-7368-3691-8 (hardcover)
    ISBN 0-7368-5171-2 (paperback)
    1. Moon—Juvenile literature. I. Title. II. First facts. Solar system.
QB582.W56 2005
523.3—dc22   2004016445

Summary: Discusses the orbit, physical characteristics, and exploration of the Moon.

Editorial Credits
Gillia Olson, editor; Juliette Peters, designer and illustrator; Jo Miller, photo researcher;
    Scott Thoms, photo editor

Photo Credits
Astronomical Society of the Pacific/NASA, 15
Corbis/Roger Ressmeyer, cover, 17
Digital Vision, 5
National Space Science Data Center, 16
Photodisc Inc., 1, 8–9, 14, images within illustrations and chart, 4, 6–7, 11, 12, 19, 21
Planetary Science Institute/William K. Hartmann, 20

1 2 3 4 5 6 10 09 08 07 06 05

Table of Contents

Walking on the Moon

The Moon has circled Earth for billions of years. On July 20, 1969, people finally landed on it. On that day, U.S. astronauts Neil Armstrong and Buzz Aldrin walked on its surface. The Moon is the only natural object in space that people have walked on besides Earth.

Fast Facts about the Moon

Diameter: 2,160 miles (3,476 kilometers)
Average Distance from Earth: 238,908 miles (384,467 kilometers)
Average High Temperature: 225 degrees Fahrenheit (107 degrees Celsius)
Average Low Temperature: minus 243 degrees Fahrenheit (minus 153 degrees Celsius)
Length of Day: 29 Earth days, 12 hours, 43 minutes
One Trip around Earth: 27 Earth days, 7 hours, 43 minutes

5

The Solar System

The Moon is Earth's **satellite**. A satellite circles another object. The planets are satellites of the Sun.

The planets circle the Sun at different distances. The rocky planets of Mercury, Venus, Earth, and Mars are close to the Sun. The gas planets Jupiter, Saturn, Neptune, and Uranus come next. Tiny, icy Pluto is farthest from the Sun.

Sun

Mercury

Venus

Earth

Moon

Mars

Jupiter

Saturn

Uranus

Pluto

Neptune

The Moon's Lack of Atmosphere

Most planets and some moons are surrounded by a layer of gases. The gases form an **atmosphere**. The Moon has no atmosphere. Without an atmosphere, the Moon has no weather and no clouds.

Fun Fact!

If you banged a drum on the Moon, you wouldn't hear it. The Moon has no air to carry the sound.

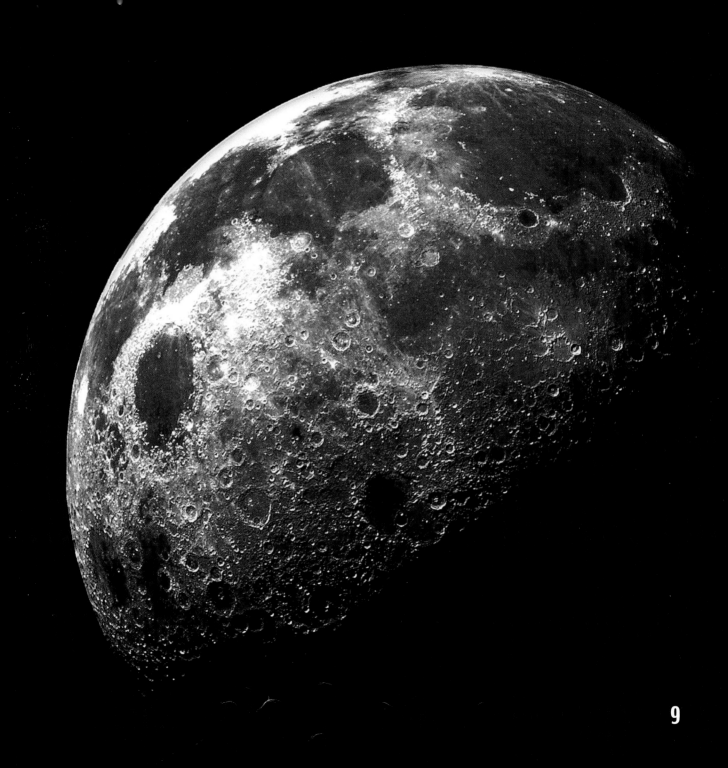

The Moon's Makeup

The Moon is made of rock and iron. The top layer of the Moon is called the crust. The crust is made of rock. Most of this rock has been crushed into dust by objects that have hit the Moon. A thick layer of rock called the **mantle** lies under the crust. Scientists think the Moon may have a small iron **core**.

Fun Fact!

Astronauts' footprints on the Moon could stay there forever. The Moon has no wind or rain to blow or wash them away.

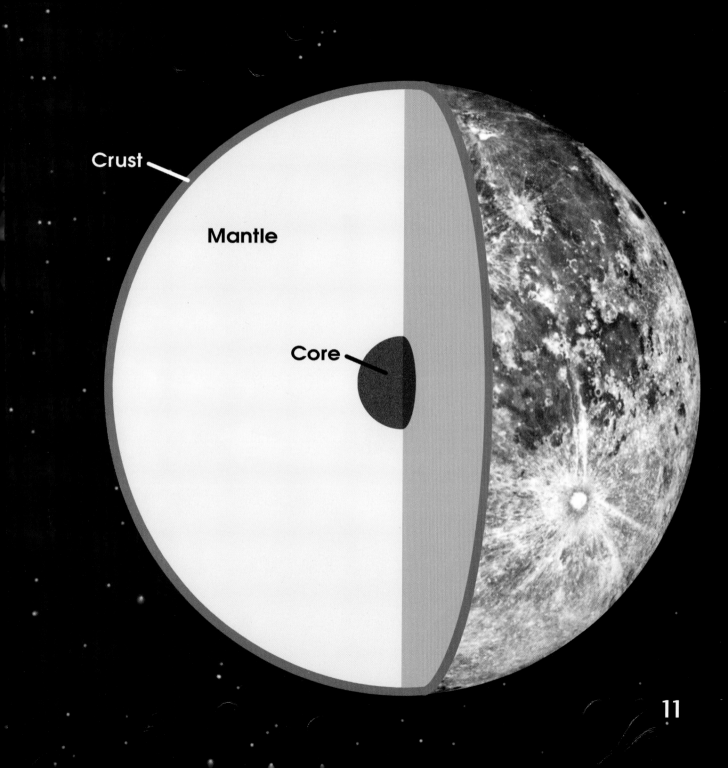

Crust

Mantle

Core

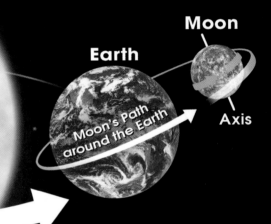

Sun

Earth's Path around the Sun

Earth

Moon

Moon's Path around the Earth

Axis

How the Moon Moves

As it moves around Earth, the Moon spins on its **axis**. It takes 27 Earth days, 7 hours, 43 minutes to spin once. The Moon makes one circle around Earth in the same amount of time. This action causes the same side of the Moon to always face Earth.

Fun Fact!
Because the Moon spins so slowly, you could almost run fast enough to keep up with the setting Sun.

Craters and Maria

Bowl-shaped **craters** dot the Moon's surface. Craters form when objects hit the Moon. One crater is larger than Canada. Others are like a pinprick in the dust.

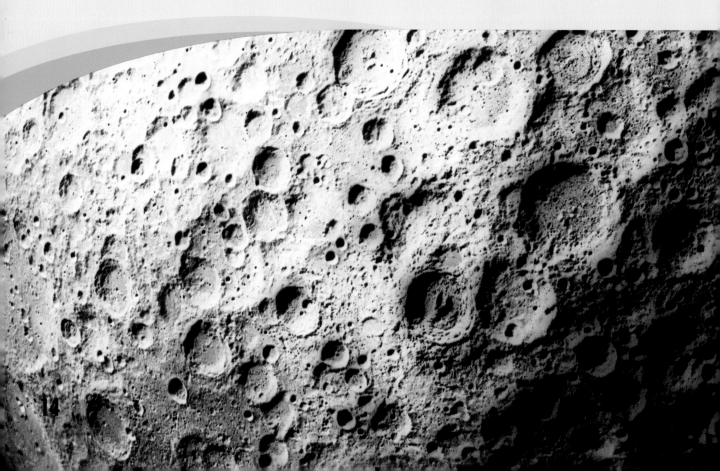

Large dark areas of the Moon are called **maria**. Lava created maria millions of years ago. The lava broke through the crust and flooded craters.

Studying the Moon

Except for Earth, the Moon is the best-known space object. Astronauts have landed on the Moon six times. They have done experiments there.

Some scientists use **lasers** to study the Moon. They have found that the Moon moves 1.5 inches (3.8 centimeters) farther away from Earth each year.

Comparing the Moon to Earth

Earth and the Moon have many differences. The Moon is much smaller than Earth. It gets much hotter and much colder. The Moon has no air for people to breathe. Still, scientists are working on ways for people to someday live on the Moon.

Fun Fact!

Astronauts brought back about 840 pounds (380 kilograms) of rocks from the Moon. These rocks help scientists compare the Moon to Earth.

Size Comparison

Earth

Moon

Amazing but True!

The Moon is probably made up of pieces of Earth. Scientists think that a planet-sized object slammed into Earth billions of years ago. This hit is called "The Big Whack." Pieces of Earth and pieces of the object flew into space. The pieces circled Earth, slowly gathering together. Eventually, the pieces formed the Moon.

Moon Phases Chart

We see the Moon because it reflects sunlight. As the Moon circles Earth, we see different amounts of the side of the Moon that is lit by sunlight. Certain points of this cycle are called phases. One cycle of phases takes 29 days and 12 hours.

People use the words waxing and waning to describe Moon phases. A waxing Moon is becoming full. A waning Moon is becoming a new Moon.

Waxing crescent
The lit part we see is shaped like a crescent.

Waxing half Moon

Waxing gibbous
Gibbous means humpbacked.

Full Moon

Waning gibbous

Waning half Moon

Waning crescent

New Moon
The fully shadowed side of the Moon faces Earth.

Glossary

atmosphere (AT-muhss-feehr)—the layer of gases that surrounds some planets and moons

axis (AK-siss)—an imaginary line that runs through the middle of a planet or moon

core (KOR)—the inner part of a planet that usually is made of metal or rock

crater (KRAY-tur)—a hole made when objects crash into a planet or moon's surface

laser (LAY-zur)—a powerful beam of light

mantle (MAN-tuhl)—the part of a planet or moon between the crust and the core

maria (MAHR-ee-uh)—large dark areas on the Moon caused by lava that flooded craters

satellite (SAT-uh-lite)—a moon or other object that travels around another object in space

Read More

Rau, Dana Meachen. *Moon.* Our Solar System. Minneapolis: Compass Point Books, 2003.

Simon, Seymour. *The Moon.* New York: Simon & Schuster Books for Young Readers, 2003.

Whitehouse, Patricia. *Moon.* Space Explorer. Chicago: Heinemann Library, 2004.

Internet Sites

FactHound offers a safe, fun way to find Internet sites related to this book. All of the sites on FactHound have been researched by our staff.

Here's how:
1. Visit *www.facthound.com*
2. Type in this special code **0736836918** for age-appropriate sites. Or enter a search word related to this book for a more general search.
3. Click on the **Fetch It** button.

FactHound will fetch the best sites for you!

Index